The

DALAI LAMA'S

Book of

WISDOM

Thorsons

Thorsons
An Imprint of HarperCollins*Publishers*
77-85 Fulham Palace Road,
Hammersmith, London W6 8JB

The Thorsons website Address is: www.thorsons.com

Published by Thorsons 1999

20 19 18 17 16 15

Buddha motif by Rochelle Green

A catalogue record for this book is
available from the British Library

ISBN 0 7225 3955 X

Printed and bound by Martins the Printers,
Berwick-upon-Tweed

THE DALAI LAMA'S BOOK OF WISDOM

CONTENTS

FOREWORD

The Book of Wisdom is an extract from the earlier publication of *Power of Compassion* – teachings by His Holiness the Dalai Lama given in May 1993 in London.

It is hoped that this extract – *The Book of Wisdom* – will bring His Holiness the Dalai Lama's message about the importance of love, compassion and forgiveness to a wider audience.

His Holiness the Dalai Lama is the spiritual and temporal leader of the Tibetan people. In 1989 His Holiness the Dalai Lama was awarded the Nobel Peace Prize for his non-violent struggle for the liberation of Tibet. Since 1959 His Holiness has been living in exile in India. Tibet continues to be occupied by Communist China.

The Office of Tibet, London

September 1999

~

I am a Buddhist and my whole way of training is according to the Buddhist teaching or Buddha *Dharma*. Although I speak from my own experience, I feel that no one has the right to impose his or her beliefs on another person. I will not propose to you that my way is best. The decision is up to you. If you find some point which may be suitable for you, then you can carry out experiments for yourself. If you find that it is of no use, then you can discard it.

His Holiness the XIV Dalai Lama

~

PART ONE

CONTENTMENT, JOY AND LIVING WELL

~

The basic fact is that all sentient beings, particularly human beings, want happiness and do not want pain and suffering. On those grounds, we have every right to be happy and to use different methods or means to overcome suffering and to achieve happier lives. It is worthwhile to think seriously about the positive and negative consequences of these methods. You should be aware that there are differences between short-term interest and long-term interest and consequences – and the long-term interest is more important. Buddhists usually say that there is no absolute and that everything is relative. So we must judge according to the circumstances.

~

~

Our experiences and feelings are mainly related to our bodies and our minds. We know from our daily experience that mental happiness is beneficial. For instance, though two people may face the same kind of tragedy, one person may face it more easily than the other due to his or her mental attitude.

~

~

I believe that if someone really wants a happy life then it is very important to pursue both internal and external means; in other words, mental development and material development. One could also say 'spiritual development', but when I say 'spiritual' I do not necessarily mean any kind of religious faith. When I use the word 'spiritual' I mean basic human good qualities. These are: human affection, a sense of involvement, honesty, discipline and human intelligence properly guided by good motivation. We have all these qualities from birth; they do not come to us later in our lives.

~

~

As humans, we all have the same human potential, unless there is some sort of retarded brain function. The wonderful human brain is the source of our strength and the source of our future, provided we utilize it in the right direction. If we use the brilliant human mind in the wrong way, it is really a disaster.

~

~

I think human beings are the superior sentient beings on this planet. Humans have the potential not only to create happy lives for themselves, but also to help other beings. We have a natural creative ability and it is very important to realize this.

~

~

With the realization of one's own potential and self-confidence in one's ability, one can build a better world. According to my own experience, self-confidence is very important. That sort of confidence is not a blind one; it is an awareness of one's own potential. On that basis, human beings can transform themselves by increasing the good qualities and reducing the negative qualities.

~

~

The fundamental teaching of the Buddha is his teaching on the Four Noble Truths: 1) That there is suffering; 2) that suffering has cause; 3) that there is cessation of suffering; and, 4) that there is a path to such freedom. The underlying principle of this teaching is the universal principle of causality. What becomes important in the understanding of this basic teaching is a genuine awareness of one's own potentials and the need to utilize them to their fullest. Seen in this light, every human action becomes significant.

~

~

It is my belief that the human brain and basic human compassion are by nature in some kind of balance. Sometimes, when we grow up, we may neglect human affection and simply concentrate on the human brain, thus losing the balance. It is then that disasters and unwelcome things happen.

~

~

The smile is a very important feature of the human face. But because of human intelligence, even that good part of human nature can be used in the wrong way, such as sarcastic smiles or diplomatic smiles, which only serve to create suspicion. I feel that a genuine, affectionate smile is very important in our day-to-day lives. How one creates that smile largely depends on one's own attitude. It is illogical to expect smiles from others if one does not smile oneself. Therefore, one can see that many things depend on one's own behaviour.

~

~

The important thing is to use human intelligence and judgement, and to be mindful of the benefits for long-term and short-term happiness. Up to a certain point, the body itself is a good indicator. For instance, if some sort of food causes you discomfort one day, then later you will not want to consume that type of food. It seems that at a certain stage the body itself can tell us what is suitable for well-being and happiness and what is not.

~

~

Sometimes your intelligence may oppose your immediate desire because it knows the long-term consequences. Thus, the role of intelligence is to determine the positive and negative potential of an event or factor which could have both positive and negative results. It is the role of intelligence, with the full awareness that is provided by education, to judge and accordingly utilize the potential for one's own benefit or well-being.

~

~

If we examine our mental world, we find that there are various mental factors which have both positive and negative aspects. For instance, we can look at two types which are quite similar: one is self-confidence and the other is conceit or pride. Both of them are similar in that they are uplifting states of mind which give you a certain degree of confidence and boldness. But conceit and pride tend to lead to more negative consequences, whereas self-confidence tends to lead to more positive consequences.

~

~

I usually make a distinction between different types of ego. One type of ego is self-cherishing in order to get some benefit for itself, disregarding the rights of others. This is the negative ego. Another ego says, 'I must be a good human being. I must serve. I must take full responsibility.' That kind of strong feeling of 'I' or self opposes some of our negative emotions.

~

~

So there are two types of ego, and wisdom or intelligence makes a distinction. Similarly, we must be able to distinguish between genuine humility and a lack of confidence. One may mistake the two because both of these are sort of slightly humbling mental functions, but one is positive and the other is negative.

~

~

There is both positive and negative desire. For instance, the Mahayana Buddhist literature mentions two desires or two aspirations. One is the aspiration to be of benefit to all sentient beings and the other is the aspiration to attain fully the Enlightened state for that purpose. Without these two types of aspiration, the attainment of full Enlightenment is impossible. But there are also negative things which result from desire. The antidote to this negative desire is contentment. There are always extremes, but the middle way is the proper way.

~

~

The sense of contentment is a key factor for attaining happiness. Bodily health, material wealth and companions and friends are three factors for happiness. Contentment is the key that will determine the outcome of your relations with all three of these factors.

~

~

When our attitude towards our material possessions and wealth is not proper, it can lead to an extreme attachment towards such things as our property, houses and belongings. This can lead to an inability to feel contented. If that happens, then one will always remain in a state of dissatisfaction, always wanting more. In a way, one is then really poor, because the suffering of poverty is the suffering of wanting something and feeling the lack of it.

~

~

Now when we talk about objects of enjoyment or desire and material well-being, Buddhist literature mentions five types of objects of desire: form, sound, odours, tastes and tactile sensations. Whether or not these objects of enjoyment give rise to happiness, satisfaction and contentment, or conversely, give rise to suffering and dissatisfaction depends very much on how you apply your faculty of intelligence. Our behaviour in our daily lives is the key factor in determining whether these really produce genuine, long-lasting satisfaction or not. Much depends on our own attitude. And for this mental factor, motivation is the key thing.

~

~

In Buddhist literature, human life is seen as a favourable form of existence or rebirth. There are various factors that could complement the favourable existence as a human being, such as having a long life, good health, material possessions and eloquence so that one can relate to others in a more beneficial way. But whether or not these conditions lead to a more beneficial existence or a more harmful one depends very much on how you utilize them and whether or not you apply the faculty of intelligence.

~

~

Buddhist literature mentions practice of the Six Perfections. For instance, in the case of acquiring material possessions, according to Buddhism, generosity and the act of giving are seen as causes of wealth. But in order to practise generosity and giving successfully, one must first of all have a sound ethical discipline. And that ethical discipline can come about only if one has the ability to bear hardships when confronted with them. For that you also need a certain degree of joyful effort.

~

~

In order to practise the application of joyful effort successfully, one must have the ability to concentrate, to focus on events, actions or goals. That in turn depends on whether or not you have the ability to exercise your power of judgement, to judge between what is desirable and what is undesirable, what is negative and what is positive.

~

How do we go about implementing in our daily lives the principles which are stipulated in the practice of the Six Perfections? Buddhism recommends living one's life within the ethical discipline of observance of what are known as the Ten Precepts, or Avoidance of the Ten Negative Actions. Most of the Negative Actions are common denominators of all religious traditions. They are seen as negative or undesirable for society in general, regardless of any religious point of view.

~

Good conduct is the way in which life becomes more meaningful, more constructive and more peaceful. For this, much depends on our own behaviour and our mental attitude.

~

PART TWO

FACING DEATH
AND DYING

~

The issue of facing death in a peaceful manner is a very difficult one. According to common sense, there seem to be two ways of dealing with the problem and the suffering. The first is simply to try to avoid the problem, to put it out of your mind, even though the reality of that problem is still there and it is not minimized. Another way of dealing with this issue is to look directly at the problem and analyse it, make it familiar to you and make it clear that it is a part of all our lives.

~

Illness happens. It is not something exceptional; it is part of nature and a fact of life. Of course we have every right to avoid illness and pain, but in spite of that effort, when illness happens it is better to accept it. While you should make every effort to cure it as soon as possible, you should have no extra mental burden. As the great Indian scholar Shantideva has said: 'If there is a way to overcome the suffering, then there is no need to worry; if there is no way to overcome the suffering, then there is no use in worrying.' That kind of rational attitude is quite useful.

~

Death is a part of all our lives. Whether we like it or not, it is bound to happen. Instead of avoiding thinking about it, it is better to understand its meaning. We all have the same body, the same human flesh, and therefore we will all die. There is a big difference, of course, between natural death and accidental death, but basically death will come sooner or later. If from the beginning your attitude is, 'Yes, death is part of our lives', then it may be easier to face.

~

~

There are two distinct approaches to dealing with a problem. One is to simply avoid it by not thinking about it. The other, which is much more effective, is to face it directly so that you are already conscious of it. Generally there are two types of problem or suffering: with one type, it is possible that, by adopting a certain attitude, one will be able to actually reduce the force and level of suffering and anxiety. However, there could be other types of problems and suffering for which adopting a certain type of attitude and way of thinking may not necessarily reduce the level of suffering, but which would still prepare you to face it.

~

~

When unfortunate things happen in our lives there are two possible results. One possibility is mental unrest, anxiety, fear, doubt, frustration and eventually depression, and, in the worst case, even suicide. That's one way. The other possibility is that because of that tragic experience you become more realistic, you become closer to reality. With the power of investigation, the tragic experience may make you stronger and increase your self-confidence and self-reliance. The unfortunate event can be a source of inner strength.

~

~

The success of our lives and our future depends on our motivation and determination or self-confidence. Through difficult experiences, life sometimes becomes more meaningful. If you look at people who, from the beginning of their lives, have had everything, you may see that when small things happen they soon lose hope or grow irritated. Others have developed stronger mental attitudes as a result of their hardships.

~

~

I think the person who has had more experience of hardships can stand more firmly in the face of problems than the person who has never experienced suffering. From this angle then, some suffering can be a good lesson for life.

~

~

Personally, I have lost my country and, worse still, in my country there has been a lot of destruction, suffering and unhappiness. I have spent not only the majority of my life but also the best part of my life outside Tibet. If you think of this from that angle alone, there is hardly anything that is positive. But from another angle, you can see that because of these unfortunate things I have had another type of freedom, such as the opportunity of meeting different people from different traditions and also of meeting scientists from different fields. From those experiences my life has been enriched and I have learned many valuable things. So my tragic experiences have also had some valuable aspects.

~

~

Looking at problems from different angles actually lessens the mental burden. From the Buddhist viewpoint, every event has many aspects and naturally one event can be viewed from many, many different angles. It is very rare or almost impossible that an event can be negative from all points of view. Therefore, it is useful when something happens to try to look at it from different angles and then you can see the positive or beneficial aspects. Moreover, if something happens, it is very useful immediately to make a comparison with some other event or with the events of other people or other nations. This is also very helpful in sustaining your peace of mind.

~

~

I will now explain, as a Buddhist monk, how to deal with death. Buddha taught the principles of the Four Noble Truths, the first of which is the Truth of Suffering. The Truth of Suffering is taught within the context of three characteristics of existence, the first being impermanence. When talking about the nature of impermanence we must bear in mind that there are two levels. One is the coarse level, which is quite obvious and is the cessation of the continuation of a life or an event. But the impermanent nature which is being taught in relation to the Four Noble Truths refers to the more subtle aspect of impermanence, which is the transitory nature of existence.

~

~

By reflecting on the coarser levels of impermanence one will be able to confront and counteract grasping at permanence or eternal existence of one's own identity or self, because it is grasping at permanence that forces us to cling onto this very 'now-ness' or matters of one's lifetime alone. By releasing the grip of this grasping and enduring within us, we will be in a better position to appreciate the value of working for our future lifetimes.

~

~

One of the reasons why awareness of death and imper-manence is so crucial in the Buddhist religious practice is that it is considered that your state of mind at the time of death has a very great effect on determining what form of rebirth you might take. Whether it is a positive state of mind or a negative one will have a great effect. Therefore, Buddhist religious practice greatly emphasizes the importance of the awareness of death and impermanence.

~

~

One of the positive side-effects of maintaining a very high degree of awareness of death is that it will prepare the individual to such an extent that, when the individual actually faces death, he or she will be in a better position to maintain his or her presence of mind. Especially in Tantric Buddhism, it is considered that the state of mind which one experiences at the point of death is extremely subtle and, because of the subtlety of the level of that consciousness, it also has a great power and impact upon one's mental continuum.

~

~

In Tantric practices we find a lot of emphasis placed on reflections upon the process of death, so that the individual at the time of death not only retains his or her presence of mind, but also is in a position to utilize that subtle state of consciousness effectively towards the realization of the path.

~

~

From the Tantric perspective, the entire process of existence is explained in terms of the three stages known as 'death', the 'intermediate state' and 'rebirth'. All of these three stages of existence are seen as states or manifestations of the consciousness and the energies that accompany or propel the consciousness, so that the intermediate state and rebirth are nothing other than various levels of the subtle consciousness and energy. An example of such fluctuating states can be found in our daily existence, when during the 24-hour day we go through a cycle of deep sleep, the waking period and the dream state. Our daily existence is in fact characterized by these three stages.

~

~

As death becomes something familiar to you, as you have some knowledge of its processes and can recognize its external and internal indications, you are prepared for it. According to my own experience, I still have no confidence that at the moment of death I will really implement all these practices for which I have prepared. I have no guarantee!

~

~

Sometimes when I think about death I get some kind of excitement. Instead of fear, I have a feeling of curiosity and this makes it much easier for me to accept death. Of course, my only burden if I die today is, 'Oh, what will happen to Tibet? What about Tibetan culture? What about the six million Tibetan people's rights?' This is my main concern. Otherwise, I feel almost no fear of death.

~

~

In my daily practice of prayer I visualize eight different deity yogas and eight different deaths. Perhaps when death comes all my preparation may fail. I hope not! I think these practices are mentally very helpful in dealing with death. Even if there is no next life, there is some benefit if they relieve fear. And because there is less fear, one can be more fully prepared. If you are fully prepared then, at the moment of death, you can retain your peace of mind.

~

~

I think at the time of death a peaceful mind is essential no matter what you believe in, whether it is Buddhism or some other religion. At the moment of death, the individual should not seek to develop anger, hatred and so on. I think even non-believers see that it is better to pass away in a peaceful manner, it is much happier. Also, for those who believe in heaven or some other concept, it is also best to pass away peacefully with the thought of one's own God or belief in higher forces. For Buddhists and also other ancient Indian traditions, which accept the rebirth or karma theory, naturally at the time of death a virtuous state of mind is beneficial.

~

PART THREE

DEALING WITH ANGER AND EMOTION

~

Anger and hatred are two of our closest friends. When I was young I had quite a close relationship with anger. Then eventually I found a lot of disagreement with anger. By using common sense, with the help of compassion and wisdom, I now have a more powerful argument with which to defeat anger.

~

~

Perhaps there are two types of anger. One type of anger could be transformed into a positive emotion. For example, if one has a sincere compassionate motivation and concern for someone and that person does not heed one's warning about his or her actions, then there is no alternative except the use of some kind of force to stop that person's misdeeds.

~

~

According to my experience, it is clear that if each individual makes an effort then he or she can change. Of course, change is not immediate and it takes a lot of time. In order to change and deal with emotions it is crucial to analyse which thoughts are useful, constructive and of benefit to us. I mean mainly those thoughts which make us calmer, more relaxed and which give us peace of mind, versus those thoughts which create uneasiness, fear and frustration.

~

~

Within the body there are billions of different particles. Similarly, there are many different thoughts and a variety of states of mind. It is wise to take a close look into the world of your mind and to make the distinction between beneficial and harmful states of mind. Once you can recognize the value of good states of mind, you can increase or foster them.

~

~

Buddha taught the principles of the Four Noble Truths and these form the foundation of the Buddha *Dharma*. The Third Noble Truth is cessation. In this context cessation means the state of mind or mental quality which, through practice and effort, ceases all the negative emotions. It is a state in which the individual has reached a perfected state of mind which is free from the effects of various afflictive and negative emotions and thoughts.

~

~

The state of true cessation is, according to Buddhism, the refuge that all practising Buddhists seek. The reason one seeks refuge in the Buddha, is not because Buddha was from the beginning a special person, but because Buddha realized the state of true cessation.

~

~

Generally speaking, in Buddhist literature, a negative emotion or thought is defined as 'a state which causes disturbance within one's mind'. These afflictive emotions and thoughts are factors that create unhappiness and turmoil within us. Emotion in general is not necessarily something negative. At a scientific conference which I attended along with many psychologists and neuro-scientists, it was concluded that even Buddhas have emotion, according to the definition of emotion found in various scientific disciplines. So *karuna* (infinite compassion or kindness) can be described as a kind of emotion.

~

~

Naturally emotions can be positive and negative. However, when talking about anger, etc., we are dealing with negative emotions. Negative emotions are those which immediately create some kind of unhappiness or uneasiness and which, in the long run, create certain actions. Those actions ultimately lead to harm to others and this brings pain or suffering to oneself. This is what we mean by negative emotions.

~

~

In Tantric practice there are meditative techniques which enable the transformation of the energy of anger. This is the reason behind the wrathful deities. On the basis of compassionate motivation, anger may in some cases be useful because it gives us extra energy and enables us to act swiftly. However, anger usually leads to hatred and hatred is always negative. Hatred harbours ill will.

~

~

I usually analyse anger on two levels: on the basic human level and on the Buddhist level. From the human level, without any reference to a religious tradition or ideology, we can look at the sources of our happiness: good health, material facilities and good companions. Now from the stand-point of health, negative emotions such as hatred are very bad.

~

~

Your mental state should always remain calm. Even if some anxiety occurs, as it is bound to in life, you should always be calm. Like a wave, which rises from the water and dissolves back into the water, these disturbances are very short, so they should not affect your basic mental attitude. If you remain calm your blood pressure and so on remains more normal and as a result your health will improve.

~

~

Some of my close friends have high blood pressure, yet they never come near to having crises in their health and they never feel tired. Over the years I have met some very good practitioners. Meanwhile, there are other friends who have great material comfort yet, when we start to talk, after the initial few nice words, they begin to complain and grieve. In spite of their material prosperity, these people do not have calm or peaceful minds. As a result, they are always worrying about their digestion, their sleep, everything! Therefore it is clear that mental calmness is a very important factor for good health.

~

~

The second source of happiness comes from our material facilities. Sometimes when I wake up in the early morning, if my mood is not very good, then when I look at my watch I feel uncomfortable because of my mood. Then on other days, due perhaps to the previous day's experience, when I wake up my mood is pleasant and peaceful. At that time, when I look at my watch I see it as extraordinarily beautiful. Yet it is the same watch, isn't it? The difference comes from mental attitude. Whether our use of our material facilities provides genuine satisfaction or not depends on our mental attitude.

~

~

It is bad for our material possessions if our mind is dominated by anger. To speak again from my own experience, when I was young I sometimes repaired watches. I tried and failed many times. Sometimes I would lose my patience and hit the watch! During those moments, my anger altered my whole attitude and afterwards I felt very sorry for my actions. If my goal was to repair the watch, then why did I hit it on the table? Again you can see how one's mental attitude is crucial in order to utilize material facilities for one's own genuine satisfaction or benefit.

~

~

The third source of happiness is our companions. It is obvious that when you are mentally calm you are honest and open-minded. Even if there is a big difference of opinion, you can communicate on a human level. You can put aside these different opinions and communicate as human beings. I think that is one way to create positive feelings in other people's minds.

~

~

I think that there is more value in genuine human feeling than in status and so on. I am just a simple human being. Through my experience and mental discipline, a certain new attitude has developed. This is nothing special. You, who I think have had a better education and more experience than myself, have more potential to change within yourself. I come from a small village with no modern education and no deep awareness of the world. Also, from the age of 15 or 16 I had an unthinkable sort of burden.

~

~

Each of you should feel that you have great potential and that, with self-confidence and a little more effort, change really is possible if you want it. If you feel that your present way of life is unpleasant or has some difficulties, then don't look at these negative things. See the positive side, the potential, and make an effort.

~

~

So, as far as our contact with fellow human beings is concerned, our mental attitude is very crucial. Even for a non-believer, just a simple honest being, the ultimate source of happiness is in our mental attitude. Even if you have good health, material facilities used in the proper way and good relations with other human beings, the main cause of a happy life is within.

~

~

Now you can see how to minimize anger and hatred. First, it is extremely important to realize the negativeness of these emotions in general, particularly hatred. I consider hatred to be the ultimate enemy. By 'enemy' I mean the person or factor which directly or indirectly destroys our interest. Our interest is that which ultimately creates happiness.

~

~

We can also speak of the external enemy. For example, in my own case, our Chinese brothers and sisters are destroying Tibetan rights and, in that way, more suffering and anxiety develops. But no matter how forceful this is, it cannot destroy the supreme source of my happiness, which is my calmness of mind. This is something an external enemy cannot destroy. Our country can be invaded, our possessions can be destroyed, our friends can be killed, but these are secondary for our mental happiness. The ultimate source of my mental happiness is my peace of mind. Nothing can destroy this except my own anger.

~

Moreover, you can escape or hide from an external enemy and sometimes you can even cheat the enemy. For example, if there is someone who disturbs my peace of my mind, I can escape by locking my door and sitting quietly alone. But I cannot do that with anger! Wherever I go, it is always there. Even though I have locked my room, the anger is still inside. Unless you adopt a certain method, there is no possibility of escape. Therefore, hatred or anger – and here I mean negative anger – is ultimately the real destroyer of my peace of mind and is therefore my true enemy.

~

Some people believe that to suppress emotions is not good, that it is much better to let it out. I think there are differences between various negative emotions. For example, with frustration, there is a certain frustration which develops as a result of past events. Sometimes if you hide these negative events, such as sexual abuse, then consciously or unconsciously this creates problems. Therefore, in this case it is much better to express the frustration and let it out.

~

~

However, according to our experience with anger, if you do not make an attempt to reduce it, it will remain with you and even increase. Then even with small incidents you will immediately get angry. Once you try to control or discipline your anger, then eventually even big events will not cause anger.

~

~

When anger comes there is one important technique to help you keep your peace of mind. You should not become dissatisfied or frustrated, because this is the cause of anger and hatred. There is a natural connection between cause and effect. Once certain causes and conditions are fully met it is extremely difficult to prevent that causal process from coming to fruition. It is crucial to examine the situation so that at a very early stage one is able to put a stop to the causal process. Then it does not continue to an advanced stage.

~

~

In the Buddhist text *A Guide to the Bodhisattva Way of Life*, the great scholar Shantideva mentions that it is very important to ensure that a person does not get into a situation which leads to dissatisfaction, because dissatisfaction is the seed of anger. This means that one must adopt a certain outlook towards one's material possessions, towards one's companions and friends, and towards various situations.

~

~

Our feelings of dissatisfaction, unhappiness, loss of hope and so forth are in fact related to all phenomena. If we do not adopt the right outlook, it is possible that anything and everything could cause us frustration. Yet phenomena are part of reality and we are subject to the laws of existence. So this leaves us only one option: to change our own attitude. By bringing about a change in our outlook towards things and events, all phenomena can become friends or sources of happiness, instead of becoming enemies or sources of frustration.

~

~

In one way, having an enemy is very bad. It disturbs our mental peace and destroys some of our good things. But if we look at it from another angle, only an enemy gives us the opportunity to practise patience. No one else provides us with the opportunity for tolerance. Since we do not know the majority of the five billion human beings on this earth, therefore the majority of people do not give us an opportunity to show tolerance or patience either. Only those people whom we know and who create problems for us really provide us with a good opportunity to practise tolerance and patience.

~

~

Shantideva says that it is the very intention of harming us which makes the enemy very special. If the enemy had no intention of harming us, then we would not classify that person as an enemy, therefore our attitude would be completely different. It is his or her very intention of harming us which makes that person an enemy and because of that the enemy provides us with an opportunity to practise tolerance and patience. Therefore an enemy is indeed a precious teacher. By thinking along these lines you can eventually reduce the negative mental emotions, particularly hatred.

~

~

Another question is that if you always remain humble then others may take advantage of you and how should you react? It is quite simple: you should act with wisdom or common sense, without anger and hatred. If the situation is such that you need some sort of action on your part, you can, without anger, take a counter-measure. In fact, such actions which follow true wisdom rather than anger are in reality more effective. A counter-measure taken in the midst of anger may often go wrong. Without anger and without hatred, we can manage more effectively.

~

~

There is another type of practice of tolerance which involves consciously taking on the sufferings of others. I am thinking of situations in which, by engaging in certain activities, we are aware of the hardships, difficulties and problems that are involved in the short term, but are convinced that such actions will have a very beneficial long-term effect. Because of our attitude and our commitment and wish to bring about that long-term benefit, we sometimes consciously and deliberately take upon ourselves the hardships and problems that are involved in the short term.

~

~

I am quite sure that if this Fourteenth Dalai Lama smiled less, perhaps I would have fewer friends in various places. My attitude towards other people is to always look at them from the human level. On that level, whether president, queen or beggar, there is no difference, provided that there is genuine human feeling with a genuine human smile of affection.

~

PART FOUR

GIVING AND RECEIVING

A practical way of
directing love and
compassion

Compassion is the most wonderful and precious thing. When we talk about compassion, it is encouraging to note that basic human nature is, I believe, compassionate and gentle. For example, one scientist has told me that the first few weeks after birth is the most important period, for during that time the child's brain is enlarging. During that period, the mother's touch or that of someone who is acting like a mother is crucial. This shows that even though the child may not realize who is who, it somehow physically needs someone else's affection. Without that, it is very damaging for the healthy development of the brain.

~

When we go to a hospital, irrespective of the doctor's quality, if the doctor shows genuine feeling and deep concern for us, and if he or she smiles, then we feel OK. But if the doctor shows little human affection, then even though he or she may be a very great expert, we may feel unsure and nervous. This is human nature.

~

~

In education, it is my experience that those lessons which we learn from teachers who are not just good, but who also show affection for the student, go deep into our minds. Lessons from other sorts of teachers may not. Although you may be compelled to study and may fear the teacher, the lessons may not sink in. Much depends on the affection from the teacher.

~

~

When we are young and again when we are old, we depend heavily on the affection of others. Between these stages we usually feel that we can do everything without help from others and that other people's affection is simply not important. But at this stage I think it is very important to keep deep human affection.

~

~

When people in a big town or city feel lonely, this does not mean that they lack human companions, but rather that they lack human affection. As a result of this, their mental health eventually becomes very poor. On the other hand, those people who grow up in an atmosphere of human affection have a much more positive and gentle development of their bodies, their minds and their behaviour.

~

~

Children who have grown up lacking a positive atmosphere usually have more negative attitudes. This very clearly shows the basic human nature. Also, as I have mentioned, the human body appreciates peace of mind. Things that are disturbing to us have a very bad effect upon our health. This shows that the whole structure of our health is such that it is suited to an atmosphere of human affection. Therefore, our potential for compassion is there. The only issue is whether or not we realize this and utilize it.

~

~

The basic aim of my explanation is to show that by nature we are compassionate, that compassion is something very necessary and something which we can develop. It is important to know the exact meaning of compassion. The Buddhist interpretation is that genuine compassion is based on a clear acceptance or recognition that others, like oneself, want happiness and have the right to overcome suffering. On that basis one develops some kind of concern about the welfare of others, irrespective of their attitude to oneself. That is compassion.

~

Your love and compassion towards your friends is in many cases actually attachment. This feeling is not based on the realization that all beings have an equal right to be happy and to overcome suffering. Instead, it is based on the idea that something is 'mine', 'my friend' or something good for 'me'. That is attachment. Thus, when the person's attitude towards you changes, your feeling of closeness immediately disappears. With the other way, you develop some kind of concern irrespective, of the other person's attitude to you, simply because that person is a fellow human being and has every right to overcome suffering. Whether that person remains neutral to you or even becomes your enemy, your concern should remain.

~

Actually genuine compassion and attachment are contradictory. According to Buddhist practice, to develop genuine compassion you must first practise the meditation of equalization and equanimity, detaching oneself from those people who are very close to you. Then, you must remove negative feelings towards your enemies. All sentient beings should be looked on as equal. On that basis, you can gradually develop genuine compassion for all of them.

~

~

It must be said that genuine compassion is not like pity or a feeling that others are somehow lower than you. Rather, with genuine compassion you view others as more important than yourself.

~

~

In order to generate genuine compassion, first of all one must go through the training of equanimity. This becomes very important because without a sense of equanimity towards all, one's feelings towards others will be biased. So now I will give you a brief example of a Buddhist meditative training on developing equanimity. You should think about, first, a small group of people whom you know, such as your friends and relatives, towards whom you have attachment. Second, you should think about some people to whom you feel totally indifferent. And third, think about some people whom you dislike.

~

~

Once you have imagined these different people, you should try to let your mind go into its natural state and see how it would normally respond to an encounter with these people. You will notice that your natural reaction would be that of attachment towards your friends, that of dislike towards the people whom you consider your enemies and that of total indifference towards those whom you consider neutral. Then you should try to question yourself.

~

~

You should compare the effects of the two opposing attitudes you have towards your friends and your enemies, and see why you should have such fluctuating states of mind towards these two different groups of people. You should see what effects such reactions have on your mind and try to see the futility of relating to them in such an extreme manner.

~

~

I have already discussed the pros and cons of harbouring hatred and generating anger towards enemies, and I have also spoken a little about the defects of being extremely attached towards friends and so on. You should reflect upon this and then try to minimize your strong emotions towards these two opposing groups of people. Then most importantly, you should reflect on the fundamental equality between yourself and all other sentient beings.

~

Just as you have the instinctive natural desire to be happy and overcome suffering, so do all sentient beings; just as you have the right to fulful this innate aspiration, so do all sentient beings. So on what exact grounds do you discriminate?

~

If we look at humanity as a whole, we are social animals. Moreover, the structures of the modern economy, education and so on, illustrate that the world has become a smaller place and that we heavily depend on one another. Under such circumstances, I think the only option is to live and work together harmoniously and keep in our minds the interest of the whole of humanity. That is the only outlook and way we must adopt for our survival.

~

~

By nature, especially as a human being, my interests are not independent of others. My happiness depends on others' happiness. So when I see happy people, automatically I also feel a little bit happier than when I see people in a difficult situation. For example, when we see pictures on television which show people starving in Somalia, including old people and young children then we automatically feel sad, regardless of whether that sadness can lead to some kind of active help or not.

~

~

In our daily lives we are now utilizing many good facilities, including things like air-conditioned houses. All these things or facilities became possible, not because of ourselves, but because of many other people's direct or indirect involvement. Everything comes together. It is impossible to return to the way of life of a few centuries ago, when we depended on simple instruments, not all these machines. It is very clear to us that the facilities that we are enjoying now are the products of the activities of many people.

~

~

Since we all have an equal right to be happy and since we are all linked to one another, no matter how important an individual is, logically the interest of the other five billion people on the planet is more important than that of one single person. By thinking along these lines, you can eventually develop a sense of global responsibility. Modern environmental problems, such as depletion of the ozone layer, also clearly show us the need for world co-operation. It seems that with development, the whole world has become much smaller, but the human consciousness is still lagging behind.

~

~

A wider or more altruistic attitude is very relevant in today's world. If we look at the situation from various angles, such as the complexity and inter-connectedness of the nature of modern existence, then we will gradually notice a change in our outlook, so that when we say 'others' and when we think of others, we will no longer dismiss them as something that is irrelevant to us. We will no longer feel indifferent.

~

~

If you think only of yourself, if you forget the rights and well-being of others, or, worse still, if you exploit others, ultimately you will lose. You will have no friends who will show concern for your well-being. Moreover, if a tragedy befalls you, instead of feeling concerned, others might even secretly rejoice. By contrast, if an individual is compassionate and altruistic, and has the interests of others in mind, then irrespective of whether that person knows a lot of people, wherever that person moves, he or she will immediately make friends. And when that person faces a tragedy, there will be plenty of people who will come to help.

~

~

A true friendship develops on the basis of human affection, not money or power. Of course, due to your power or wealth, more people may approach you with big smiles or gifts. But deep down these are not real friends of yours; these are friends of your wealth or power. As long as your fortune remains, then these people will often approach you. But when your fortunes decline, they will no longer be there. With this type of friend, nobody will make a sincere effort to help you if you need it. That is the reality.

~

~

Genuine human friendship is on the basis of human affection, irrespective of your position. Therefore, the more you show concern about the welfare and rights of others, the more you are a genuine friend. The more you remain open and sincere, then ultimately more benefits will come to you. If you forget or do not bother about others, then eventually you will lose your own benefit.

~

~

There are various positive side effects of enhancing one's feeling of compassion. One of them is that the greater the force of your compassion, the greater your resilience in confronting hardships and your ability to transform them into more positive conditions.

~

One form of practice that seems to be quite effective in enhancing compassion is found in *A Guide to the Bodhisattva Way of Life*, a classic Buddhist text. In this practice you visualize your old self, the embodiment of self-centredness, selfishness and so on, and then visualize a group of people who represent the masses of other sentient beings. Then you adopt a third person's point of view as a neutral, unbiased observer and make a comparative assessment of the value, the interests and then the importance of these two groups. You will naturally begin to feel more inclined towards the countless others.

~

I also think that the greater the force of your altruistic attitude towards sentient beings, the more courageous you become. The greater your courage, the less you feel prone to discouragement and loss of hope. Therefore, compassion is also a source of inner strength.

~

~

With increased inner strength it is possible to develop firm determination and with determination there is a greater chance of success, no matter what obstacles there may be. On the other hand, if you feel hesitation, fear and lack of self-confidence, then often you will develop a pessimistic attitude. I consider that to be the real seed of failure. Therefore, even in the conventional sense, compassion is very important for a successful future.

~

~

Having reflected upon the faults of a self-centred way of thinking and life, and also having reflected upon the positive consequences of being mindful of the well-being of other sentient beings and working for their benefit, and being convinced of this, then in Buddhist meditation there is a special training which is known as 'the practice of Giving and Taking'. Using visualization, it basically involves taking upon yourself all the suffering pain, negativity and undesirable experiences of other sentient beings.

~

~

You imagine taking this suffering upon yourself and then giving away or sharing with others your own positive qualities, such as your virtuous states of mind, your positive energy, your wealth, your happiness and so forth. Such a form of training, psychologically brings about a transformation in your mind so effectively that your feeling of love and compassion is much more enhanced.

~

~

One thing you should remember is that mental transformations take time and are not easy. I think some people from the West, where technology is so good, think that everything is automatic. You should not expect this spiritual transformation to take place within a short period; that is impossible. Keep it in your mind and make a constant effort, then after 1 year, 5 years, 10 years, 15 years, you will eventually find some change. I still sometimes find it very difficult to practice these things. However, I really do believe that these practices are extremely useful.

~

~

My favourite quotation from Shantideva's book is: 'As long as space endures, as long as sentient beings remain, until then, may I too remain and dispel the miseries of the world.'

~